Table of Contents

Chapter 1: Affirmations for Success 1

Chapter 2: Affirmations for Luck 6

Chapter 3: Affirmations for Work 9

Chapter 4: Affirmations for Positive Thinking 12

Chapter 5: Affirmations for Self-Esteem 15

Chapter 6: Affirmations for Wealth 18

Chapter 7: Affirmations for Good Health 20

Chapter 8: Affirmations for Intelligence 23

Chapter 9: Affirmations for Healing 26

Chapter 10: Affirmations for Spirituality 29

Chapter 11: Affirmations for Love 32

Chapter 12: Affirmations for Cleanliness 35

Chapter 13: Affirmations for Strength 37

Chapter 1:
Affirmations for Success

We all need help with building up our self-esteem for success and these affirmations will help you do just that.

Affirmations for Success:

I am an extremely successful person.

I wake up each and every day to accomplish great things

I believe that success comes with hard work

I am a hard-working and successful person

I am one of the most successful people to ever exist

I believe in achieving great things

I have great goals in life and will accomplish them

I believe in being an extremely successful person

I love being who I am

I love and enjoy everything about myself

Look to this book for positive and great affirmations to help guide you through everyday life and to help give you a more positive viewpoint of things. This book will help you with transforming your mind and allowing it to reprogram into better thought patterns.

It's important in life to think positively and to have an incredibly positive state of mind. Sometimes its not always easy to do this due to the nature of working, lethargy, trauma, the need to heal and many other factors in life. It's important to energize your brain and mind with positive amazing thoughts that will help heal you and help transform your mind into a machine of goodness and positive happy thinking. These affirmations are one important way of healing your mind and energizing yourself and helping you become a more whole, one and happy person in life.

Affirmations are a powerful tool for self-improvement and personal growth. They can be used to focus on positive thoughts that counteract negative beliefs or feelings, build self-confidence, and help you stay motivated towards your goals. Affirmations can be incorporated into daily life by taking time to practice them out loud or in writing every day, repeating them during difficult times to access your inner strength, and visualizing the outcomes of these affirmations becoming true.

Using affirmations is a simple but powerful process. Start by identifying an area in your life that you would like to focus on, then think of an affirmation or mantra related to it. Repeat them out loud multiple times each day. This will help reprogram your brain and create new habits of thought which can improve how we feel about ourselves and our lives. They can assist us with easing of pain, overcoming past trauma, and improving our lives. They help with healing and a vast number of other life related subjects and should be a part of our daily routine, lifestyle, and way of thinking.

Repeat these affirmations to yourself several times a day and watch them help you manifest your life into a better and happier one! Enjoy your greatest transformation!

It's imperative that we focus on what is positive and train our minds into thinking happy and positive thoughts and ideas. Once these thoughts become embedded into our subconscious minds, they begin to transform our way of living and thinking and allow more positive experiences to take place. These affirmations will help build your self esteem, your way of thinking and will change your life!

I am an extremely accomplished person

I have achieved many successes in life

I believe that true success comes with being an accomplished person

I love to work hard and achieve my goals

I believe in hard work and dedication

I am a strong and independent person

I am strong and successful

I am independent and hard-working

I motivate myself to accomplish my goals

I am a dedicated and motivated person

I have the ability to motivate myself

I am enough and great

My talents are unique and special

I dedicate myself to doing great things

I am a very accomplished and successful person

I am a rich and wealthy person who has everything I need

A little progress each day can add up to great results

I am a strong and successful person

I am strong successful and beautiful

I am a beautiful person

I am wonderful and positive

I am a positive person

I choose good over evil

I choose good over negativity

I go against any and all negativity

I seek to be happy healthy

I love myself more every single day

I possess unrequited goodness and beauty

I'm an inspirational person to everyone

I can accomplish anything I so desire

I am the best at any job I do

Success comes easy to me

I never compare myself to others

I am the most successful person I know

I am becoming more successful everyday

I am proud of myself and my successes

I am happy with my current successes

Today is a great day for me

Everyday is a successful day for me

I am becoming more successful each and every day

I wake up every morning energized and ready to go

I am ready to face the wonderful day ahead

I am a truly successful and accomplished person

I am a powerful person and am in charge of my destiny

I am in charge of my life and destiny

I make worthy contributions to the world

I am surrounded by a positive support group of people

I believe in myself and my successes

I feel I can do anything I want

I enjoy my life and live it to the fullest

I continue to climb higher on the ladder of success

I have great goals in life and plan to achieve them

I celebrate every beautiful aspect of my life

I am a good person

I love myself

I am grateful for everything I own and possess

I am a very grateful happy person

I can manifest anything in my universe

I can make anything happen that I want to

I can make any good thing happen

I am the controller of my world

I control my world and actions

I manifest all my dreams and accomplishments to come true

I wish only good for others

I have no envy or jealousy for others

I only possess great qualities of goodness and love

I possess an abundance of joy and happiness

I am the manifester of all great things in my world

I only manifest good and abundant things in my life

I take control of my dreams and make them come true

I can make all of my goals and dreams come true

I have wonderful great goals and dreams and they will come true

My dreams in life are very important

I am an important person

I have important things to do with my time

I contribute to this world in a great way

I am a powerful force on this planet

My talents are recognized by others

I am a powerful and important person

Great things have happened to me

I have the power to manifest anything I put my mind to

Chapter 2:

Affirmations for Luck

We all want to be lucky, and this chapter helps you out with luck and allows you to feel and believe in your own good luck and personal power

Affirmations for Luck:

Good luck comes my way at all times

People tell me im very lucky

Im one of the luckiest people out there

I do great at everything I take part in

Money comes my way very easily

I always do well in the lottery

Good luck always comes to me

I feel lucky all the time

I am a happy go lucky person

Im lucky at my job

Good things are always happening to me

I am lucky in love and find it easily

Good luck is my best friend

Great Luck always finds me wherever I go

I expect good luck in everything I do

Bad luck never comes my way

Good luck is my best friend

I am the luckiest person in the world

Why am I so happy and lucky?

Im very lucky with when I meet someone

im very lucky with the ladies

I get very lucky when I meet a man

Im so lucky in love, it flocks to me

No one can be as lucky as me

Good luck is always by my side

I am a privileged and lucky human being

I am the luckiest person on the planet

Good things happen to me all the time

I am so happy with all the good things happening to me

Women love my presence and want my attention

Men love my presence and want my attention all the time

I am such a lucky human being

I attract good luck in every aspect of my life

I am very lucky in everything that I do

I can easily meet my soulmate

Very good luck always comes my way

Ive never had trouble with bad luck

I am the luckiest happiest person

I am open to receiving luck and fortune in my life

My outlook is filled with positive energy, inviting more good luck into my life

The universe lavishes me with its blessings of good luck and abundance

Luck finds its way to me when I least expect it

I know that the best kind of luck comes from taking action and trusting in myself

Chapter 3:
Affirmations for Work

If you need a boost with your job and some confidence, these affirmations can help with this and help get you going everyday

Affirmations for Work:

I matter

My work matters

I am successful at any job

I am the best at any job I do

I am the most successful worker out there

I am a very hard worker

I work harder and smarter than most people

I have the best job you can find

I am one of the hardest workers

I love to work and be productive

I love going to my job

I enjoy working and find it fun

My job is rewarding and worthwhile

My job is fun

I have a very important job

Any kind of work I do is important and matters

I love working for such a good company

I love my boss and enjoy their company

My boss is my good friend

My co-workers all respect me and enjoy my company

My job is very important and worthy of accolades

I go to a very important job every day

I am very lucky to be able to work and have a job

Working is fun and gives me something worthy to do

I love learning new things.

I enjoy taking instruction and learning and improving

I feel important when I do my work

I am doing worthwhile important work for my company

I work for a prestigious and very good company

I am motivated to be the best at my job

I am determined to do the best job I can ever do

I am the hardest worker at my job

I am very successful at my work

I deserve a very good promotion

I possess a great amount of power and wealth

I make very good money and do well at my job

I earn a very good income

I love what I do everyday

I enjoy spreading joy to others

I rarely make mistakes and if I do I learn from them

I find opportunity in every experience I have

I gain experience and growth from everything I do

I am a very talented person who deserves good pay

I deserve bonuses and good pay

I possess many great talents and my company is lucky to have me

Every ounce of my being is full of worthy achievements

Going to work everyday is a great achievement

I enjoy learning new things and growing

I love taking instruction and improving at what I do

I am the best employee at my work

I am proud of my achievements and efforts

My talents and efforts are worthy

I am hardworking and motivated to succeed in my career

My focus and determination help me reach my goals with ease

Success comes naturally when I put forth effort and dedication

I have the courage to take risks that can lead to greater rewards

Opportunities come to me through commitment and perseverance

I find myself accomplishing more each and everyday

My work is important to me

I believe in the importance of any task that I accomplish

Chapter 4:

Affirmations for Positive Thinking

Positive thinking is really important. We need to have positive and good thoughts in order to reprogram our mind into thinking good things and allowing good effects to take place in our life

Affirmations for happiness and positive thinking:

I love myself unconditionally

I am a beautiful special person

I love being a good and happy person

I seek to do only good deeds and actions

My words are positive and beautiful

I speak only the truth

I speak and live only positivity

I love being myself

People love to be in my wonderful company

I have a great and bubbly personality

I have a beautiful personality

I am a very intelligent person who people love to be around

I seek to better myself each and everyday

I love myself each and every day more

Im a positive happy person

I am a special person

I enjoy helping others out

My friends and family enjoy my company

Others love my company

I am a wonderful caring person

I am a kind good person

I am a beautiful kind and precious soul

I believe in being kind to animals and people

I believe in utter and total kindness to every living being

I believe in being an extremely positive and good person

I am a patient and happy person

I will share the word of God with anyone who will listen

I have a deep spiritual belief in goodness and kindness

I love myself and am free from other people's judgments

I replace negativity with only positive beliefs and outcomes

I choose to be a loving and kind individual

I am full of happiness and bliss only

I am in control of everything that happens in my life

I am one of the most amazing people to exist

Its ok to make mistakes and I gladly admit any of my shortcomings

I love being myself and being me

I am proud of the accomplishments I've had

I am proud of who I am

I have the best self esteem

I think very highly of myself

I approve of myself and every good thing I have done

I seek to only do good deeds

I love doing positive and good deeds

I love making others happy

I enjoy making other people smile

I enjoy being loving caring and kind to animals

Being a positive person is easy for me

I love being a positive and happy person

I enjoy spreading joy to others

I am a very compassionate person

I am a confident person

I am constantly thinking of positive thoughts to bring myself up

Happy positive thoughts and ideas make who I am

I breathe and sleep positivity and love

I am positive and giving

I am a caring loving person

I love giving my kindness to others

Chapter 5:

Affirmations for Self-Esteem

It's important to be a person who believes in yourself, and this is what this chapter is full of- the attributes of being the kind of amazing person who believes in yourself

Affirmations for self-esteem:

I always do the right thing

I am excellent company to be around

Only good things happen to me

Good and great things come my way

Positive and loving people come into my life

I care about others deeply

I have great self esteem

I heal myself each and everyday

I have a deep and positive connection to those around me

I believe in doing good and beautiful deeds

I think it's important to be kind to everyone

I believe good karma will come my way

I don't care how others perceive me

I'm a wonderful person who is kind and giving

You're such a beautiful person

You're so wonderful and special

You are special and great

You are amazing

youre too good for people out there

Many people are too insecure to handle someone better than them

You are above others

You have better self-esteem than others

You are higher and greater than other people

Never let others bring you down

You are worthy of love and relationships

I don't let others judge or bother me

Never allow others to judge or bring you down

You are so special and worthy

You are one of God's greatest most wonderful creations

God loves you very much

You are worthy of great love and affection

I love to cook, and try new and different things

I am an eclectic and amazing person with many talents and gifts

I am a passionate and amazing person

I have a deep passion for many things in life

People love to be in my company

Everyone loves to be my friend and wants to be my friend

I possess great charisma

I am loved by everyone around me

Everyone who encounters my presence witnesses my importance

I am worthy of love and affection

I am worthy of praise and accolades

I have a family that loves me greatly

I have many friends that love me

Everyone loves my presence and attention

I am a blessing to anyone whose presence I encounter

You are a wonderful, talented special amazing person

You deserve only the best

You deserve to be treated the very best

No one's opinion matters, only yours

It doesn't matter what others think of you

I am capable, confident and worthy of all that I desire

My worth is determined by me alone, not by the opinions of others

I embrace my flaws and see them as part of what makes me unique

I love myself unconditionally and accept all parts of who I am

My mistakes do not define me, I can learn from them and grow to be better than before

Chapter 6:
Affirmations for Wealth

These affirmations will help bring money your way and keep it coming. This will help you gain greater wealth and come into more money in life

Affirmations for wealth:

I am an incredibly wealthy person

Money comes my way very easily

I can easily be rich if I want to be

I am a rich person with a lot of money

People flock to me and love my presence

I have a charismatic and amazing presence

I possess great amounts of wealth and charisma

Im very lucky when I play the lottery

Money easily comes to me

I do well at my job and make great money

I am one of the wealthiest people

I attract wealth and abundance into my life

My financial situation is always improving

I am guided towards success in all of my endeavors

My financial flow increases daily

Every day, I become more financially secure and independent

I open myself up to an endless supply of wealth and abundance

My financial life is filled with success and growth

I am confident in my ability to create my own prosperity

Money comes easily and effortlessly into my life

My finances reflect the joy, abundance, and security I desire

I always create more and more wealth

Financial prosperity is a part of my life

I am wealthy beyond my wildest dreams

My future holds unlimited potential for creating wealth

I trust in the universe to provide me with all I need to become wealthy and abundant

I am financially secure and capable of achieving my financial goals

My hard work will allow me to build a stable financial future

Financial abundance is within my reach

I can easily create great wealth for myself

Opportunities for unlimited wealth are always coming to me

I can always manifest great abundance of wealth into my life

I am a financially prosperous person

I have an abundance of wealth

Chapter 7:

Affirmations for Good Health

These affirmations will help you lose weight and stay healthy overall and have great health. You always want to stay in perfect and good health and it's important to have that right state of mind to help you achieve this

Affirmations for good health

I am always in very good health

My health is perfect

I eat very healthy and know exactly what my body wants

I eat to nourish my beautiful body and make sure it stays healthy

I only eat healthy foods that will help my body flourish

I love to eat healthy and nourish my body

I nourish my body with healthy foods

I eat to nourish every cell in my body

Every cell in my body is full of love and light

I know exactly what to eat to stay healthy

My body is a beautiful temple

Only healthy and nourishing foods can enter my body

I enjoy eating extremely healthy

I have a passion for keeping my body healthy and nourished properly

Everything I eat promotes good health

It's easy for me to lose weight

I can eat healthy and lose weight easily

I don't consider myself overweight

I am the perfect weight and height

I look great and wonderful

My overall health is really good

I possess great health and feel great

I can easily keep my weight level

I am very thin and beautiful

I look wonderful and am beautiful

I have no issue with keeping a healthy weight

No one can bring me down

I am always in great health

I am beautiful and worthy of self-care

I have the power to nourish my body with healthy foods and exercise

I can always find balance between health and indulgence

I have the power to create a healthy lifestyle for myself

I can reach optimal wellbeing for myself at any time

I trust that good health is always possible

I can beat any issue or health problem

I am beautiful and special

I have a beautiful body that im proud of

Chapter 8:
Affirmations for Intelligence

These affirmations and words will help boost your confidence and self-esteem when it comes to your great intelligence and will help you be a more confident person

Affirmations for Intelligence:

I possess an unlimited amount of wisdom and knowledge

I am an extremely intelligent and knowledgeable person

I am highly gifted and brilliant

I am the most intelligent person on the planet

I am a genius, and can accomplish anything I want

My brain is a genius and gifted, and my talents are limitless

There is no limit to what I can accomplish in life

I am one of the smartest people I know

I am an intelligent person who has the capacity to learn and grow

I am one of the most intelligent people on the planet

My brain is very unique and I am a gift

I know things many people do not know

I know a lot about many things

I am a master of intellect

I am an academic intellectual

I can do anything I put my mind to

I can achieve anything I want to

I can go to any college or school I so desire

I can accomplish any difficult task

My mental capacity has no limits

I am a gifted genius

My mind is very unique and brilliant

I am a very brilliant person

I was blessed with a very beautiful amazing mind

I am an extremely smart intelligent blessed person

I am much smarter than I think I am

I am capable of far more than I think I can do

I can think on my toes

I have a very quick and intelligent mind

I can think very fast

I win almost any game I play

I can win every game I play

I am competitive and brilliant

I am the smartest person I know

I am a capable person

I think very quickly

My mind is unique and smart

I am very talented

I possess a rare intelligent mind

I am a deep thinker

I am a philosopher and intellectual

I love being intelligent and smart

I love being incredibly smart

I enjoy difficult trivia games

I can be accomplished in any field I want

I possess a very creative mind

I can write any kind of book I want

I can write a book if I so wish

My mind is a powerful tool I use to accomplish anything I desire

I can do anything I so desire

My mind is inquisitive and creative, allowing me to think outside of the box

I have the power to take on any challenge with a confident attitude

My intelligence will lead me to great success

I am a smart and capable person, who is constantly learning and growing

Because of my great intellect, I can take on any challenge with confidence

Chapter 9:

Affirmations for Healing

These wonderful words will help you heal faster and better and allow your natural self-healing processes to take place

Affirmations for healing:

I let go of any negativity or trauma that is holding me back

My fears will be replaced with love love and abundance

I seek to better myself and become a better person

I can finally achieve true happiness

I am a forgiving and loving person

Money comes my way very easily

I can easily meet my soulmate

My soulmate is out there somewhere searching for me

I can find love and happiness very easily

I can easily let the past go

I seek to attain a higher level of awareness

I have a strong belief in God and a higher force out there

I believe God loves me greatly

I can easily heal and let go of the past

Healing comes very easily to me

I let go of any past traumas that have troubled or held me back

I love myself unconditionally

I can easily heal from the past

I can easily let go of anything from the past

I am full of happiness love and positivity

I am a great person who can achieve great things

I have achieved and accomplished great things

I can easily heal within myself any past situations

I contemplate in beauty love and perfection

Healing comes easily and naturally to me

I can heal easily

I have a natural capability to heal and let go

I refuse to trauma bond in any way

I am full of love light and healing energy

I wont let the past hold me back or bring me down

I wont let others bring me down

I am fully confident in myself and believe in myself

I believe in all of my attributes

I am a determined and hard working individual

I am worthy of health and happiness

My body is capable of naturally restoring itself to its optimal state

I trust in the power of self-care and nourishment

The universe always provides what I need for my healing journey

I embrace positivity, which helps me heal from within

I am worthy and deserving of love and healing

My body is strong and resilient, capable of recovering from any setback

Each day I am becoming stronger than before

I will trust in the process of healing, allowing it to take its course naturally

I am grateful for my health and well-being.

I have the power to heal myself of anything

I am resilient and strong and capable of overcoming any challenge

Chapter 10:
Affirmations for Spirituality

These affirmations will help you in your spiritual path and help you become a more spiritual person

Affirmations for spirituality:

I immerse myself in perfect harmony love and peace

I am an incredibly peaceful person

I am full of tranquility beauty and love

You are braver and stronger than you think you are

You are capable of things greater than you believe you are

You possess qualities and greatness that you do not yet know of

I only think positive healthy and beautiful thoughts

Spirituality is a part of my essence and soul

My soul is full of beauty love and light

You possess wonderful capabilities you do not know of

I can do anything I set my mind to

I can do anything I want and possess great capabilities

Inspiration is the key to achieving anything we want to

I am an honest and good person

I breathe goodness love and positivity

You can achieve anything you want, if you try hard enough

Life is a wonderful beautiful gift and journey to be explored

Animals are beautiful and wonderful companions and friends

Animals should only be treated with great kindness and respect

I give importance to every living being I encounter

I understand the importance of every living being

I believe in the beautiful and wonderful gift of life

Love is the essence of true goodness

I am full of great positivity and love

I am good at everything I do

I treat every living being with extreme respect and importance

I possess an abundance of love and light

I believe in being a good and humble soul

I believe in being against anything evil

I am humble and not arrogant

I can create great wealth if I want to

I create goodness and love wherever I go

My spirit is beautiful and amazing

I have a great and beautiful soul

I am satisfied with being a great happy soul

I am full of goodness and peace

I am an extremely peaceful, happy person

Joy and love radiate from me

I am filled with beauty, love and joy

Goodness and peace radiate from me

I am a spiritual and deep thinker.

I am a philosophical and deep person

I am a deeply spiritual and gifted person

My soul is full of extreme light energy

I am full of light and love energy

I believe in doing only good and positive deeds

I enjoy and love helping others

I love helping and healing others

I enjoy being kind to animals

I am connected to a greater spiritual force that inspires and guides me

My spirit is powerful, compassionate and open-minded

I allow myself to find inner peace no matter what happens in life

I trust that my great spirit will lead the way

I create harmony in my life through faith and mindfulness

I make the most out of every moment

I enjoy living in the present moment

Chapter 11:

Affirmations for Love

These words will help you with your luck in love and help you attract love in all areas of life

Affirmations for beauty and love:

I am beautiful, wonderful and special

Everyone is madly in love with me

Anyone who graces my presence falls in love with me

I possess a beauty and presence that is uncomparable

Many different people are attracted to me

My significant other is madly in love with me

My significant other is greatly attracted to me

My spouse wants to be with me only and loves me

Women flock to me and love my presence

Men find me attractive and want to be with me

I am very lucky in love

I can easily find many people to be with

I can find my soulmate easily

I am an extremely passionate person

I am loyal loving caring and forgiving

My significant other can count on me to be loyal and trusting

I am a passionate lover

I am a passionate and amazing significant other

Whoever is with me is blessed

Anyone is blessed to be my lover and partner

I am worthy of unconditional and lasting love.

My heart is open to receive the deepest kind of love

I attract healthy, fulfilling relationships into my life

Love is a source of strength in my life that never fades away

I trust in the universe to bring me beautiful connections and relationships

My heart is capable of giving and receiving the greatest kind of love

I am open to experiencing a new level of joy, connection, and passion in my relationships

I let go of all fear and accept only pure love into my life

Love comes effortlessly into my life when I give it freely to others

I can trust that true love awaits me when I am ready for it

I have the potential to love deeply and unconditionally

I enjoy inundating those around me with warmth and kindness

I embrace love in all aspects of my life

I love to be loved and show it to those around me

I can attract all kinds of wonderful love into my life

I can give and receive love freely

My relationships are full of joy and understanding

I am a kind caring and giving person

I have a wonderful heart that is full of love and joy

I am a wonderful blessing to be around

I am a great kind and caring lover

I deserve to be loved

People flock to me and want my attention and company

I enjoy loving others and being loved

Love is a beautiful blessing in my life

I possess an abundance of love in my heart

I deserve to have great love in my life

Chapter 12:

Affirmations for Cleanliness

It's important to be clean and to have affirmations that help us with staying as neat and tidy as possible

Affirmations for cleanliness:

I love cleanliness and love a clean home

I am a neat freak

People count on me to be very tidy and clean

I love being a clean and neat person

I smell really good

Im a clean friendly and neat person

I love to have a clean and nice home

My car is very clean and nice

All my rooms are clean

My bedroom is neat and nice looking

I have a very clean and nice appearance

I enjoy showering daily

I love to take long showers and stay clean

Being clean is important to me

I enjoy smelling nice

My living room is very clean and smells nice

I cant stand filth or dirtiness

I appear very well kempt and neat

I don't want to appear to be a slob to others

I enjoy being very neat and tidying up anywhere I go

I take pride in taking care of my physical environment

I create a healthy and hygienic space to live, work, and play

My commitment to tidiness allows me to enjoy a clutter free life

Organization helps me stay focused on the tasks at hand

Cleanliness brings peace of mind and clarity into my life

With a little effort, I can create a refreshing atmosphere

I have the power to create order in my home

Being clean and neat takes little effort for me

Chapter 13:
Affirmations for Strength

We all need affirmations to give us strength and to bring our inner strength out. These words will help guide you into becoming a stronger and more resilient person.

Affirmations for strength:

I am the strongest person in my universe

I possess great strength

I possess the strength of thousands of people

I am a survivor

I am one of the strongest people I've ever known

I am the greatest success I know

I rarely compare myself to others

I am satisfied with being who I am

I am a strong willed and good person

I am an honest person

I have great character

I am a strong-willed person

My strength is uncomparable

I am constantly growing

I am relieved and free From any pain

I have a beautiful body

I love my body

I see what's inside a person

I am in greater peace every second of my existence

I have the power to manifest what I desire

I surround myself with positive helpful people

I never put down or judge others

My desires and needs are important

I am a critical part of this planet.

My thoughts and opinions are worthy

My presence and opinion are valuable

I am an inspiration to those around me

People look up to me

I am an inspiration to everyone

I can do anything I put my mind to

My strength is unparalleled

Im stronger than most people

I am the strongest person I know

I have the strength to overcome adversity

I have incredible strength

I will not let anyone control my life

I have power and strength over others

I am an incredibly powerful person

I have great power and strength

I am healing and strengthening myself every single day

I am strong and capable of anything I set my mind to

My inner power grows with every challenge I face

I have the courage and resilience to overcome any obstacle in life

My spirit is unbreakable, no matter what comes my way

I trust that I have all the strength within me to make it through hard times

I am powerful and capable of achieving great things

I trust in my own strength and resilience

I believe in myself and the decisions I make

My voice is important and I will use it to speak up for what I believe in

I am determined to succeed, no matter what obstacles come my way

I am in control of my own destiny

I have the courage to make difficult decisions

My potential is limitless, and I will strive to reach it

My personal power is unbreakable and I'm proud of who I am

I will never give up on myself or my goals

I can manifest anything my wonderful heart desires

I am strong, capable and powerful

I have the ability to make wise decisions and take control of my life

I possess the courage to persevere and reach success

My power and strength will always lead the way

I can manifest anything I so desire

Great things will happen to me

www.ingramcontent.com/pod-product-compliance
Lightning Source LLC
LaVergne TN
LVHW010439070526
838199LV00066B/6094